A Miscellany of

Garden Wisdom

A hybrid of classic and contemporary
tips for the budding gardener

Isobel Carlson

summersdale

A MISCELLANY OF GARDEN WISDOM

Copyright © Summersdale Publishers Ltd, 2005
Additional text by Jayne Robinson and Duncan Rumney

Summersdale Publishers Ltd
46 West Street
Chichester
West Sussex
PO19 1RP
UK

www.summersdale.com

Printed and bound in Great Britain

ISBN 1 84024 467 4

Contents

Introduction

Whether you're an unseasoned gardener or your knowledge is already ripe, this collection of classic and contemporary tips will be a source of inspiration.

Overflowing with practical advice on coping with every aspect of gardening, as well as more unusual tips such as microwaving daffodil bulbs and watering your house plants with coffee, this book also contains snippets of fascinating garden folklore and unique planning techniques.

Our garden wisdom is handily divided into easy to use sections, to make sure that you and your garden reach your most blissful potential.

The journey to becoming a gardening guru will not be easy. But with a little assistance and a sprinkle of garden magic, you can battle the bugs and the slugs, and plant, prune and dig your way to your very own paradise.

Read on to follow the (garden) path to green-fingered enlightenment...

Planning Your Paradise

*'The garden must first be prepared in
the soul or else it will not flourish.'*

English proverb

WHEN IT COMES to planning a garden, size really
does matter! Don't design a garden that is too big
for your plot. Bigger is not necessarily better – just
remember that everything should fit into the space
easily and naturally.

❋ ❋ ❋

BEFORE PLANNING YOUR garden it is important to
work out what direction your garden faces, as the
amount of sunlight that it receives can affect the
layout and types of plants that you can grow. You
should also make a note of the areas that get a lot
of sunlight and those that get more shade.

ARRANGE YOUR PLANTS according to their watering requirements to save you valuable time in the future.

✿ ✿ ✿

WHEN PLANTING, TAKE into account a plant's size at maturity. Layer by height and bloom time for emphasis and constant colour.

✿ ✿ ✿

MAKE A SMALL garden feel larger by putting bright, attention-grabbing colours at the front of a border and cooler colours at the back.

If your garden is dark
and shady, bring in light
by painting your fences
white and using reflective
surfaces to make the
most of any sunlight.

WHEN LAYING OUT paths in small gardens, create an illusion of space by narrowing the walkway as it continues down the garden from the house. Make the end of the path about a foot narrower than the start of the path and watch your guests marvel!

Garden Lore...

Yellow flowers in the garden will protect the whole family from witches.

Sorting your Yin from your Yang

'How fair is a garden amid the trials and passions of existence.'

Benjamin Disraeli

WHEN DESIGNING YOUR garden, bear in mind the three basic concepts of Feng Shui:

Energy flow is a very important factor.

Wavy or curvy lines are beneficial.

Straight lines are negative.

AIM FOR AN equal balance of yin (dark, soft, passive) and yang (light, hard, active).

✿ ✿ ✿

THERE ARE GENERATIVE and destructive relationships between the five elements: wood, fire, earth, metal and water.

✿ ✿ ✿

NORTH IS THE direction of personal growth and creativity. Use water elements such as ponds and fountains in the north of your garden, but avoid stone, clay and earth here.

In the east, the direction
of new life and growth,
incorporate wood elements:
columns and cylinders such
as trees or wooden posts.
Avoid metal and white
flowers in this space.

THE NORTH-EAST IS the direction of wisdom and nature, so use aspects of the earth element here. Keep surfaces low and flat and include stone benches, paving stones and rock gardens.

❀ ❀ ❀

YOU SHOULD ALSO use wood elements in the south-east, which is the direction of wealth and communication. This is a good area to cultivate and display plants and flowers for shows.

THE SOUTH IS the direction of dreams, aspirations and happiness, and is represented by the fire element. Incorporate pointed and triangular shapes here, and barbecues or lights. Avoid water elements.

❈ ❈ ❈

IN THE SOUTH-WEST, the area of marriage, romance and motherhood, include low flat surfaces and the earth element.

❈ ❈ ❈

THE WEST, THE direction of children, creativity and entertainment, is represented by the metal element. Design your garden to incorporate an area for outdoor entertaining here, using circles and arches.

THE NORTH-WEST IS also represented by the metal element and indicates trade, travel, and interests away from home. This is a good area for statues, animals and wind chimes. Avoid barbecues and red flowers here.

Garden Lore...

Plant rowan or mountain ash outside homes and barns to protect those within from evil curses.

Tools of the Trade

*'He that would perfect his work
must first sharpen his tools.'*

Confucius

WHEN BUYING TOOLS, be sure to handle them first to check that they feel comfortable and aren't too heavy for you.

❈ ❈ ❈

KEEP YOUR TOOLS rust free and good as new by keeping an old oily rag in the garden shed and wiping them after each use.

❈ ❈ ❈

DIG OUT YOUR laddered old stockings or tights and hang them in a cool dry place – they're great for storing bulbs or onions!

INSTEAD OF BUYING expensive bamboo canes, grow your own! They look lovely in a garden, and can be harvested in the autumn and dried in a cool place. Grow them in pots or in your garden, but remember to keep them well watered and drained.

❋ ❋ ❋

MAKE YOUR GARDENING gloves last longer: when one glove wears out, wash the spare one and turn it inside out. It's then ready to be part of a new pair of gloves.

Don't throw your old potato peeler away; it's a handy gadget for removing weeds.

DON'T WORRY IF your leaky old garden hose is looking a bit worse for wear – use a sharp nail to prick a few more holes into it and *voilà*! A new sprinkler for your lawn.

✻ ✻ ✻

FILL AN OLD hot water bottle with polystyrene chips for a waterproof and wipe-clean knee cushion to make those long gardening jobs a little more comfortable.

✻ ✻ ✻

STORE YOUR TOOLS away from ground level by hanging them up – it is surprising how much moisture can come up through a shed or garage floor and rust the metal.

USE DISINFECTANT WIPES to clean your pruners between cuts to keep your plants healthy and disease-free. They're an easy and less messy alternative to a bucket of bleach and water.

※ ※ ※

USE LENGTHS OF old guttering to irrigate your vegetable patch. Drill small holes along the guttering, lay it alongside your row of vegetables and pour some water into one end.

※ ※ ※

SECATEURS ARE GREAT for dead heading or collecting flowers for arranging purposes. They can hold the flower head between the blades until the handles are released so you aren't left with dead flower heads all over the ground!

KEEP YOUR NAILS and cuticles looking as beautiful as your garden – protect them by tucking half a cotton wool ball into the fingertips of your gardening gloves.

🐾 🐾 🐾

KEEP SHOVELS, TROWELS and shears working well by regularly sharpening them with a file, but remember to wear safety goggles and leather gloves before you attempt to sharpen anything.

DON'T THROW AWAY broken crockery – use it to line the bottom of plant pots for good drainage.

Garden Lore...

The name 'foxglove' is derived from a legend which claims that evil fairies gave a fox the flower petals to put on his toes so that he could sneak into the chicken house without being heard!

The Basic Ingredients

Soil

*'To forget how to dig the earth and tend
the soil is to forget ourselves.'*

Mahatma Gandhi

ALWAYS CHECK THE pH of your soil before spending all your hard-earned cash on unsuitable plants that will struggle to grow in your garden. Invest in a simple pH testing kit from your local garden centre.

❊ ❊ ❊

HEALTHY SOIL SHOULD be home to a community of earthworms, centipedes and beetles, who help to aerate the soil and break down organic matter. Attract them by maintaining the pH level between 6.0 and 7.0, and keeping the soil well fertilised.

FIND OUT YOUR soil type by picking some up and rubbing it between your finger and thumb. If the soil blows away then it is sandy. If it clumps together then it is clay. Both soil types have their advantages. If you have recently moved to a new area, why not have a walk round and see what is growing successfully in your neighbours' gardens?

✿ ✿ ✿

SPREAD SHEEP'S WOOL around if you have clay soil – it helps to break it down, improving aeration and draining the soil. It also adds nutrients to the soil as it breaks down.

USE PLENTY OF compost on sandy soil as it will improve the texture by filling in the holes between the tiny stones of which sand is composed. This will also increase its ability to hold water and nutrients.

❋ ❋ ❋

DECOMPOSED LEATHER IS rich in nutrients so don't throw your old leather shoes away – bury them in the garden!

When you stop for a tea break, give your grass some too! Open a tea bag and sprinkle the tea on your lawn – it makes a great natural fertiliser.

STOP MOSS FROM growing all over your soil by laying a bulky organic mulch over the ground to encourage an open, well-drained soil surface.

Garden Lore...

If the bees in your garden all buzz away back to their hive, it means that rain is on its way.

Compost

*'Earth knows no desolation. She smells
regeneration in the moist breath of decay.'*

George Meredith

COMPOST IS WHAT happens when leaves, grass
clippings, vegetable and fruit scraps, woodchips,
straw and small twigs are combined and allowed
to break down into a soil-like texture. Use it instead
of commercial fertilisers wherever possible.

❀ ❀ ❀

COMPOST CAN BALANCE out both acidic and alkaline
soils so it is an ideal way to improve your soil,
whatever type you have been blessed with.

❀ ❀ ❀

TO GIVE YOUR compost a kick start, throw a few
shovelfuls of old manure, alfalfa or blood meal
over it, and then add some more during the
process as an extra boost. This will provide
the compost with plenty of bacteria, giving the
microbes energy to break down material.

SHEEP MANURE IS probably the richest source of nutrients, just ahead of horse manure. Don't bother with cow and pig manure – they're sloppy and messy and haven't really got much to offer.

❀ ❀ ❀

YOUR COMPOST PILE should be no smaller than one cubic metre, as this size pile will generate enough heat to decompose while still allowing for sufficient airflow. Invest in a compost thermometer from your local garden centre, and remember that the ideal temperature for effective composting is between 120° and 160° Fahrenheit. This heat is achieved when enzymes are effectively breaking down the molecules of the composting material.

If you want your compost heap to remain active during the cold winter, use a bin placed in the sun, or insulate the sides with hay bales to keep the compost warm.

WEED-FREE AND PESTICIDE-FREE grass clippings bring nitrogen to your compost – be sure to mix them in well to avoid smells and to get the maximum benefit from the grass.

※ ※ ※

COMPOST CAN BE made in six to eight weeks, or it can take a year or more. The more effort you put in, the quicker you get compost.

TURN YOUR COMPOST pile every two weeks for fast results. The finished compost should look and smell like rich, dark soil.

❀ ❀ ❀

DON'T ADD THESE to your compost pile: harmful charcoal or coal ashes which contain high amount of sulphur; cat or dog droppings which might contain disease; and weeds, which will only return disease back to the soil once you spread your compost.

❀ ❀ ❀

YOUR COMPOST PILE should be moist all the way through so be sure to wet each layer and add water every time you increase your pile.

ADD BIRCH LEAVES to your compost heap – they disinfect the soil and prevent fly diseases.

✿ ✿ ✿

WHEN DISTRIBUTING THE first results of your compost spread it in an area that needs the most attention and has the worst soil. This will show you the effectiveness of your compost.

✿ ✿ ✿

APPLY COMPOST TO your soil two to four weeks before new planting as this gives the compost time to integrate with the soil.

PLANTS BENEFIT MOST from compost when it is mixed thoroughly with the soil to a depth of six inches, as plants growing in a layer of pure compost will struggle to send roots down below it into the soil.

❦ ❦ ❦

ALGAE, SEAWEED, AND lake weed are good additions to your compost pile but remember to wash off the salt water before adding them to the pile.

❦ ❦ ❦

DO NOT LEAVE a finished compost pile standing unprotected, as it will lose nutrients. Special breathable compost cover sheets can be found at any garden centre.

ONCE YOU HAVE nibbled all the sweetcorn off a stalk, chop up the stalk and throw it onto the compost pile.

🌸 🌸 🌸

DON'T THROW YOUR fingernail clippings out – they make another welcome addition to the compost pile!

Garden Lore...

Mandrake is thought to have aphrodisiac and fertilising properties.

Hanging Gardens

*'A morning glory at my window satisfies me
more then the metaphysics of books.'*

Walt Whitman

WHEN USING A wire basket, line it with damp sphagnum moss before filling it with soil to give a neater appearance and stop the soil from falling through.

❀ ❀ ❀

RECYCLE AN OLD wire bicycle basket by lining and filling it with compost and flowers. Attach it to a wall to provide an interesting display piece.

❀ ❀ ❀

FOR PRACTICALITY, GROW herbs and small vegetables in a window box outside your kitchen window.

PLANT LOVELY SCENTED plants in your window boxes so that the scent wafts inside. Recommended plants include double lilacs, which flower in May and June, and the butterfly bush which flowers from July to October and as an added bonus attracts butterflies!

※ ※ ※

LAYER SOME GRAVEL around the base of the plants in your window box to prevent your windows from getting mucky when rain splashes onto the soil.

※ ※ ※

BEAR IN MIND that wooden flower boxes provide better insulation for soil and plants than plastic or metal ones.

GIVE THE SOIL some insulation and stop it from drying out by lining the box with newspaper.

❀ ❀ ❀

UNLESS YOU LIKE to live in darkness, choose low growing plants for your window box, or climbers that can be trained against the wall around the window.

❀ ❀ ❀

LAYER THE PLANTING in your window box with taller plants at the back, bushy plants along the middle, and sumptuous trailing plants (not advisable in very windy gardens!) along the front row to give that overflowing effect.

A good way to water hanging baskets is to place ice cubes on top of the soil to prevent them from dripping all over the place.

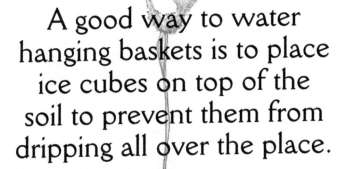

PREVENT YOUR PLANTS from becoming waterlogged by making sure that your box has drainage holes.

※ ※ ※

WHEN PLANTING A hanging basket, work from the inside out, pushing plants through the sides after carefully positioning their roots inside.

※ ※ ※

PLACE USED TEA bags in the bottom of a hanging basket before adding compost, as they make an excellent fertiliser and retain water.

TRY LINING YOUR hanging baskets with disposable nappies (clean ones mind you!). The gel will work like expensive water retaining gel crystals at a fraction of the cost.

🐾 🐾 🐾

ONE WAY TO make watering hanging baskets easier if you are, let's say, vertically challenged, is to attach a bamboo cane along the last few feet of the hose pipe to keep it rigid. This will enable you to reach those otherwise hard-to-reach places!

IF THE SOIL in your hanging baskets becomes too dry, a squirt of washing up liquid added to the water will help the water to enter the compost instead of running off.

Garden Lore...

Parsley will only grow outside the home of an honest man or a strong woman.

From the Beginning

'All the flowers of all the tomorrows
are in the seeds of today.'

Indian proverb

ENSURE EVEN DISTRIBUTION when sowing very small seeds by mixing them with a little sand in a sugar shaker or a plastic yoghurt pot with holes in the bottom.

❁ ❁ ❁

AN OLD BROOM handle is perfect for making a shallow seed trench – simply lay the handle along the soil and walk along it to press it down firmly.

❁ ❁ ❁

TIE SOME CELLOPHANE loosely around the stalk of a flowering plant to collect falling seeds.

Sow seeds between 2 p.m. and 4 p.m. to give a better rate of germination, this way the temperature-sensitive phase of the germination process is completed at night when soil temperatures are lower.

✻ ✻ ✻

Seeds with hard outer casings, such as Cannas and black-seeded varieties of sweet peas, need a little help to germinate, so try these tricks before planting: soak them in warm water for 24 hours to soften them up; or make a small cut in the seed with a sharp knife to help the fleshy part to push through. If the seeds are too small to make this possible, line a jar with sandpaper (rough side facing inwards), place the seeds inside and shake the jar until the seeds become scratched or roughened.

Use cardboard egg boxes
instead of seed trays when
growing seeds indoors
– use one compartment
for each seed. You can
then plant the box straight
into the ground, as the
cardboard will decompose.

SUNFLOWER SEEDS WILL thrive if planted around your compost heap and as an added benefit when the sunflowers grow they'll hide the unsightly heap. But make sure you leave an opening to access the compost without damaging the flowers!

※ ※ ※

DON'T THROW AWAY your squeezy lemon juice container after pancake day – keep it in the greenhouse and refill with water for watering fragile baby seedlings drop by drop without damaging them.

DON'T THROW AWAY empty seed packets. They will give you valuable information about plant height and spacing.

✼ ✼ ✼

WHEN SOWING SEEDS that you have not tried before, sow some in a separate pot to use as a reference. This way, when the seeds start to grow, you will know what to look for and will not confuse them with weeds.

PLANT BULBS AT approximately three times their depth to give them a good chance of thriving.

✿ ✿ ✿

WHEN PLANTING BULBS in the garden, first plant them inside a flowerpot and then bury the pot as this can be more easily lifted once the bulbs have grown and finished flowering.

✿ ✿ ✿

GIVE YOUR DAFFODIL bulbs a good squeeze before planting them. If the bulbs feel soft, chances are they are harbouring bulb fly lava. Don't despair – a 60-second turn in the microwave will kill all the bugs, leaving you free to plant healthy bulbs.

CHEER UP YOUR daffodils by mixing dry mustard with fertiliser when you plant the bulbs – they will turn an even brighter yellow!

✿ ✿ ✿

PLANT DAFFODIL BULBS before the end of October and tulips before the end of November.

CROCUSES LIKE SHADE so plant them in cool shady spots such as around tree bases or below hedges.

❋ ❋ ❋

TULIPS ARE SUN lovers so plant them in a sunny spot with good drainage.

❋ ❋ ❋

NEVER PLANT TULIPS and lilies together as they suffer from the same diseases and if one becomes ill then they will pass the disease onto the other.

CAT OWNERS WHO love tulips are in luck, as the mice that normally like to feast on tulip petals will be frightened off by your feline friend.

❋ ❋ ❋

DON'T PLACE MANURE near to tulips during the growing process, as it is too strong for them. Instead, use well-drained compost to nourish the bulbs before they flower.

Garden Lore...

An acorn at the window will keep lightning out.

Green, Green Grass

'Every blade of grass has its Angel that bends over it and whispers, "Grow, grow."'

The Talmud

TO ENSURE AN evenly sown lawn, divide the area into equal squares and allocate the same amount of seed for each square. Then give the area a light rake just to make sure.

❊ ❊ ❊

REFRIGERATE GRASS SEEDS for a couple of days before sowing to encourage more vigorous growth.

❊ ❊ ❊

FREQUENT MOWING ENCOURAGES lawn growth, so mow once a week when grass is growing well. Try not to mow the grass if it is growing slowly during drought periods, and do not mow grass when it is very wet.

IF YOU HAVE children or lively pets, you will need a particularly hardwearing grass.

✿ ✿ ✿

ALTHOUGH GRASS CUTTINGS left on a lawn will return goodness to the soil, they actually do more harm than good – invariably encouraging weeds.

✿ ✿ ✿

TRIM THE SIDES of your lawn neatly by laying a plank along its edges and using the sharp edge of a spade to cut the straggly edges into line.

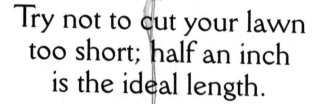

Try not to cut your lawn
too short; half an inch
is the ideal length.

IF YOUR LAWN becomes neglected and overgrown, cut the length of the grass bit by bit. The shock of a short-back-and-sides when it has been used to a mullet will render the grass less sturdy and in need of fertiliser.

✻ ✻ ✻

DETER PESKY MOLES from ruining your lawn by cutting off their food supply – they love earthworms, so invest in a worm killer and the moles will have to go to somebody else's garden for lunch!

NEVER WALK ON a frozen lawn. It will be brittle and easily damaged, and will be left with brown patches.

✾ ✾ ✾

DAFFODILS SCATTERED HAPHAZARDLY across a lawn may look lovely in the spring but they inhibit the cutting of the grass, which in turn causes the turf to deteriorate. Try planting bulbs in drifts to minimise the area of lawn affected.

TRY NOT TO water your lawn unless absolutely necessary. Once you have watered it once, the grass will expect to be watered every week but watering will encourage weeds and clover rather than grass, which is much more resilient to dry weather.

Garden Lore...

Parsley should never be given away, as misfortune will be sure to follow.

Flower Power

'The earth laughs in flowers.'

Ralph Waldo Emerson

BUILD UP A relationship with your local garden centre or nursery. They will be a good sounding board for your ideas and a great resource of information as you and your garden grow.

※ ※ ※

IF YOU ARE unsure whether a plant is hardy enough for your garden, look out for the Royal Horticultural Society Award of Garden Merit. Plants with this label have been tested and approved by the RHS.

※ ※ ※

REPLACING ANNUALS CAN become expensive so try to concentrate them in just a few places around your garden to get maximum impact without the costs.

IT'S BETTER TO use plants in your garden that are native to your area or that have been imported from areas with similar climates and soil. They will be accustomed to your environment and will need less care to stay healthy and strong.

🐝 🐝 🐝

BE WARNED – some flowers, including sweet peas, foxglove, lantana, lupines, iris, clematis, poinsettia, amaryllis and oleander, are poisonous so take extra care when handling them and keep your pets from chewing on them!

🐝 🐝 🐝

BRIGHTEN UP A shady corner of your garden with the following plants that will grow well without much sunlight – monkshood, masterwort, Christmas rose, Virginian cowslip, bugle, columbine, bergenia, lungwort and wood-lily.

DON'T PULL UP all of your nettles – they are great at stimulating the growth of their neighbouring plants and also attract butterflies.

✻ ✻ ✻

BLUEBELLS LOOK LOVELY in a garden, but English bluebells can be very invasive. For a less boisterous variety consider the Spanish bluebell, *hyacinthoides hispanica*.

To ENCOURAGE PLANTS to grow bushy rather than tall, pinch their ends tightly with your fingers.

🌺 🌺 🌺

WHEN WATERING YOUR plants, always fit a rose to the watering can to avoid washing away any nutrients or damaging young plants.

🌺 🌺 🌺

TANTALISE YOUR SENSES with sweet smelling flowers such as lily-of-the-valley, catmint, irises, violets, and some sweet peas.

TO GET PLENTY of autumn colour in your garden, plant Japanese maples, deciduous azaleas or some of the viburnums.

❦❦❦

THE COLOUR OF your hydrangea is determined by your soil pH. Blue hydrangea will turn pink when planted in neutral or alkaline soils, whereas pink and red varieties can turn blue or purple in acidic soils. If you would like to deepen the colour of your blue hydrangea, alter the pH of the soil by planting iron nails around the plant's base. If you would prefer pink, sprinkle some lime around the plant.

FROST CAN BE washed off tender plants with a gentle spray from your hosepipe or watering can.

✿ ✿ ✿

TO HELP WITH water conservation in summer months buy drought-resistant plants. Usually these plants have small silver leaves and deep taproots. Succulents such as cacti are also able to withstand dry weather.

PROTECT YOUNG SPRING plants from late frosts by planting them inside old rubber tyres, covered with a sheet of polythene. This will keep them safe and cosy until the warmer weather comes and they can be thinned out and replanted.

❋ ❋ ❋

RESIST THE TEMPTATION to plant summer bedding plants until all danger of frost has past. This is early April in the south but not until early May in northernmost parts of the country.

❋ ❋ ❋

PROTECT OUTDOOR PLANTS from frost by spraying them with cold (yes, cold!) water in the evenings. As the water evaporates, it will generate just enough heat to protect the plant from frost damage.

GET YOUR HOLLYHOCKS drunk – they love the yeast from beer!

* * *

PLACE CRUSHED EGGSHELLS under sweet pea seeds to increase your yield.

* * *

USE DISPOSABLE PLASTIC knives to label your plants to ensure that you don't forget a name or colour when the plant isn't in bloom. Write the details on the handle in marker pen and simply stick the knife into the ground next to the plant. These labels will be waterproof and last for years!

NEWLY PURCHASED FLOWERS are best planted in the late evening or on a cloudy day. Also their chance of survival is much greater if they are planted in rainy weather rather than dry sunny conditions.

❊ ❊ ❊

IF PLANTING FROM plastic containers, be sure to loosen the roots, as they will no doubt have become stuck together.

❊ ❊ ❊

PLANTS LIKE TO stick to what they know, so water plants with the same temperature of water as they're used to. If you have plants in a greenhouse, use tepid water otherwise you may damage their roots.

GOOD PLANTS FOR formal hedges are arborvitae, barberry, boxwood, hornbeam, inkberry, juniper, privet, sweet bay and yew.

❋ ❋ ❋

IF A NEW plant's label says it needs sun, that means direct sunlight for at least eight hours a day. If the label says shade, that means less than four hours of sunlight a day. 'Part sun' means four to six hours of sunlight a day.

❋ ❋ ❋

WHEN YOU DIG a hole for a new flower, throw in a handful of compost before placing the plant inside. The compost will provide nutritional support throughout the season and improve the soil structure around the plant.

If your ferns are drooping,
they are probably
starving! Add some castor
oil to their roots and
watch them perk up.

IF YOU REALLY have to move plants around out of season when the ground is cold, give your plant a little central heating by pouring hot water into the hole before planting.

✻ ✻ ✻

FOXGLOVES WILL KEEP disease away from the garden, so even if they don't fit in with your planting scheme, try to keep some in a lonely corner of your garden.

SAVE MONEY ON plant ties for smaller plants by using an old cassette- or videotape, using the cassette or video case as the dispenser. The tape is strong and won't rot.

❋ ❋ ❋

WATER YOUR PLANTS less frequently but in greater depth. Otherwise, if you water a little and often, your plants will develop shallow roots that dry out quickly when you are unable to water them.

❋ ❋ ❋

IF YOU ARE lucky enough to live near the sea, plant shrubby veronicas, escallonias, firethorns and snowberries as all of these will tolerate those salty sea breezes!

IN WINTER, FRAGILE plants can be protected with a blanket of straw, bracken or leaves, which can be held in place with gardener's netting secured with sticks.

✻ ✻ ✻

MULCH ACID LOVING plants with a thick layer of pine needles each autumn. As the needles decompose, they will increase the acidity of the soil.

Garden Lore...

Store a leek in your attic to prevent fire.

Climbing the Walls

AFTER CHRISTMAS, REMOVE the branches from your Christmas tree and use its trunk as a support for climbers like roses or clematis.

❀ ❀ ❀

FOR A BEAUTIFUL scent every time you step out of the house, try training a scented climber such as wisteria or honeysuckle around your front door.

❀ ❀ ❀

TRAIN YOUNG TRAILING plants up a wall with the help of plasticine or Blu-Tack.

REMEMBER WHEN USING trellis to train a climber up a wall that the plant needs to be able to wrap itself around the trellis, so fix the panels about two inches away from the wall. Small wooden blocks or empty reels of thread are handy for this.

✿ ✿ ✿

COVER AN UGLY fence or rusty iron roof with a Russian vine, which has lots of lovely white flowers and grows extremely quickly.

Garden Lore...

It is bad luck to kill a ladybird.

Coming up Roses

*'It will never rain roses. When we want to
have more roses, we must plant more roses.'*

George Eliot

PLANT ROSES IN November and remember to drive
the support stake into the ground before planting
the root ball to avoid damaging it.

🌸 🌸 🌸

ROSES WITH LARGE or cluster flowers should
generally be planted about twenty inches apart
so as not to restrict their growth.

🌸 🌸 🌸

IF YOU ARE intending to cover a wall with roses,
choose a climber rather than a rambler, as ramblers
are more prone to mildew. Fix wires horizontally
along the wall, about eighteen inches apart and
three inches away from the wall.

PLANTING PARSLEY NEAR to your roses brings a wealth of benefits. It will enhance the scent of your roses, encourage bees, and repel greenfly. What more could you ask for?

✽ ✽ ✽

BURY A LUMP of fat or dripping below your roses to give them a boost. Watch out for digging pets though!

✽ ✽ ✽

WHEN PLANTING YOUR rose tree, take a square of grass and place it grass downwards, in the bottom of the newly dug hole. Then simply plant your rose tree and watch it bloom.

BURY BAKED BANANA skins under the soil around your rose beds – they are full of potassium, just what roses need for vigorous growth.

✻ ✻ ✻

GARLIC IS A great help to gardeners – it cures black spot when planted around roses and protects against mildew in roses and carrots.

Garden Lore...

Ivy grown on a house protects
those inside from evil.

Flavour From Your Garden

'As rosemary is to the spirit, so lavender is to the soul.'

Anonymous

PICK HERBS JUST as they are coming into flower for maximum flavour!

✳ ✳ ✳

GATHER HERBS EARLY in the morning in dry weather, as wet herbs tend to develop mildew as they dry out.

✳ ✳ ✳

MAINTAIN COLOUR AND flavour by drying your herbs as quickly as possible after picking, but in a gentle heat with good ventilation. You can dry herbs on a baking tray in a barely warm oven, or alternatively preserve a supply in the freezer, washed and stored in a plastic bag.

STORE YOUR DRIED herbs in jars in a cool dark place. Expect their shelf life to be 1–2 years.

🐝 🐝 🐝

MINT HAS A mind of its own and will take over the garden if allowed. Keep it contained in an old washing up bowl with a couple of drainage holes sunk into the ground.

🐝 🐝 🐝

GIVE YOUR MINT an extra strong flavour by planting camomile next to it.

PLANT BASIL PLANTS with ginger root in the soil, as the basil will thrive in the company of the ginger.

※ ※ ※

GROW CHERVIL AND parsley in partial shade in the summer.

※ ※ ※

A FEW SPRIGS of herbs scattered onto the charcoal at a barbecue will give a lovely aroma while waiting for the food to cook.

LAVENDER WILL LOOK pretty and smell beautiful on those summer evenings!

✿ ✿ ✿

PARSLEY IS QUITE difficult to grow from seed, so heat up the soil with a good dousing of boiling water before sowing. This will speed up the germination process.

✿ ✿ ✿

BROAD-LEAFED PARSLEY HAS a great flavour and grows much more easily than the curly type.

FENNEL AND DILL may taste great together but they tend to cross pollinate, so keep them well apart in a herb garden.

✱ ✱ ✱

GROW MARIGOLDS AS an alternative to expensive saffron – they have a light, delicate flavour and their petals can be used to colour food.

Garden Lore....

Rosemary planted by the doorstep will keep witches away.

Terrific Trees

'Though a tree grows so high, the
falling leaves return to the root.'

Malay proverb

THE BEST TIME to plant a tree is in its dormant
period from late autumn to early spring.

❀ ❀ ❀

MAKE SURE THAT you give newly planted trees
extra water to prevent them suffering from the
shock of transplant. Water deeply on a weekly
basis during the main growing season.

❀ ❀ ❀

TAKE INTO ACCOUNT the expected growth of any
potential tree and the size of your garden.

IF YOU HAVE an exposed or windy garden, trees such as sycamore, ash, laburnum, birch, hawthorn, pine, oak and white willow will withstand the elements.

❀ ❀ ❀

IF YOU LIVE in a city where the air is more polluted, tolerant trees such as maple, horse chestnut, alder, silver birch, or poplar are your best choice.

❀ ❀ ❀

FIR AND BEECH trees prefer to live in acidic soil, whereas maple, cedar and cypress like alkaline.

GOOD TREES FOR small gardens are dwarf conifers, Japanese maple, Chinese red birch, cherry tree or aleppo pine.

✿ ✿ ✿

BEFORE PLANTING YOUR new tree make sure you loosen the roots, otherwise the tree may strangle.

✿ ✿ ✿

ASH TREES ARE very greedy and take more than their share of goodness from the soil, so it's not a good idea to plant anything else too close to them without a good dollop of fertiliser.

Use a stem guard to
protect your baby tree
from animal intruders.

PROVIDE INTEREST DURING those dull winter months by planting trees with attractive bark, such as the Himalayan birch with its silvery white bark, or the *Acer Davidii*, a maple with striking bright green and white striped bark.

❀ ❀ ❀

IF YOU WANT to hurry the decay of a tree stump, drill holes in it and fill the holes with any kind of sugar. Soak it in water and cover with a thick layer of mulch.

❀ ❀ ❀

IF YOU WOULD like to stay on good terms with your neighbours, make sure that trees do not affect their house or view.

IF A TREE from your garden overhangs your neighbour's fence and the neighbour cuts the branches back – the branches are legally yours, along with any fruit on them! However, any pesky roots that crawl under your fence and annoy your neighbour are your legal obligation.

❋ ❋ ❋

STOP SLUGS AND snails from climbing your trees by smearing Vaseline around the trunk.

Garden Lore...

Silver maples will show the lining of their leaves before a storm.

Going Potted

*'Bread feeds the body, indeed, but
flowers feed also the soul.'*

The Koran

REDUCE THE WEIGHT of a large pot by filling the lower half with empty plastic bottles and then adding compost on top. Be sure to make drainage holes in the bottles first.

✿ ✿ ✿

KEEP SNAILS AWAY from potted plants by smearing Vaseline around the edge of the pot every couple of weeks.

✿ ✿ ✿

POTTED PLANTS GROUPED together will benefit from the increased humidity. Be sure not to jam the plants so close that the leaves do not lie in a natural position, as this will effect their growth.

As STRANGE AS it seems, earthworms do occasionally manage to find their way into potted plants. Remove them easily by burying a slice of raw potato underneath the soil but close to the surface – this will draw the earthworms to one place, making them easy to remove.

※ ※ ※

USE POTS WITH a reservoir in the bottom if you do not have time to water daily. The soil can then soak up moisture from the reserves as needed.

To help keep roots cool and moist inside a plant pot, use plants with trailing foliage to shade the sides of the pot.

IF YOU USE plastic pots instead of clay pots for your potted plants, you won't have to water as often. Clay pots absorb excess soil moisture, minimising danger of over watering.

❋ ❋ ❋

IF YOU ARE using a clay pot, soak the pot in water before planting to prevent the pot from soaking up all of the plant's water.

❋ ❋ ❋

IF YOU HAVE a deck or patio plant pots with perfumed flowers such as citrus, plumeria and gardenia. This will add an extra dimension to the atmosphere on those warm summer nights.

IF YOU ARE going away for a few days fill a plastic jug with water and put one end of cotton rope in the jug and the other end in the plant pot. The rope will act as a wick taking water from the jug to the plants, keeping them happy while you are away. You can also use this trick for house plants.

❀ ❀ ❀

PLACE A FEW sheets of newspaper between spare plant pots when stacking them to prevent the pots from sticking together.

EXTENDABLE CURTAIN POLES are a perfect support for tall potted plants, as they can be lengthened as the plant grows taller.

Garden Lore...

Plant hawthorn trees as a hedgerow to keep out bad luck and mischievous spirits.

Protecting your Paradise

'Around a flowering tree, one finds many insects.'

Guinean proverb

KILL PESKY INSECTS on your prized plants by sprinkling them with the juice of the potato plant. This will also leave a smell that should repel insects in the future.

✳ ✳ ✳

SPRINKLE BROKEN EGGSHELLS around the base of vulnerable plants to deter slugs and snails.

✳ ✳ ✳

DISCOURAGE BIRDS FROM eating your flowers and fruit by hanging shiny objects such as tin foil or unwanted CDs from trees. These will flap in the wind and scare off the birds.

SPRINKLE A LITTLE boiling water over your cabbages, just for a couple of seconds, to kill cabbageworms.

✳ ✳ ✳

MAKE LITTLE HATS for your baby cabbages out of old tights or stockings to protect them from insects. As the cabbage grows, the stockings will stretch too!

✳ ✳ ✳

REMOVE EVEN THE heaviest aphid infestation by spraying infected areas first with diluted soapy water and then with clear water.

PLANT COREOPSIS, FEVERFEW and sweet alyssum in your vegetable bed to attract beneficial insects that will munch away happily on pests such as aphids and whiteflies.

❋ ❋ ❋

A GOOD WAY to trap aphids is to set a yellow dish in the garden filled with some water and oil. The aphids love the colour yellow, and once attracted the oil will stop them from escaping.

❋ ❋ ❋

SEND RABBITS HOPPING by spreading some talcum powder around their favourite plants.

KEEP YOUNG PLANTS safe from slimy intruders by cutting the bottom off a plastic bottle, and placing it over the plant. The plant will grow up through the top and slugs won't stand a chance! Don't forget to remove the cap of the bottle.

✳ ✳ ✳

TRAP SLUGS IN plastic cups planted in the ground and filled with beer or wine. The slugs will fall obligingly in and die in a happy place, and this way it's kinder to hedgehogs who have a tendency to chomp on deadly slug pellets.

✳ ✳ ✳

KEEP INSECTS AWAY from your tomato plants by placing aluminium foil underneath the plants for a few days after you transplant them into the garden. The sunshine reflected on the foil will confuse the insects that normally hide under the foliage so they will move to another area.

SCATTERING BLOOD AND bone around certain areas of the garden is a good way to deter rabbits. Not for the vegetarians amongst you!

✳ ✳ ✳

IF YOU ARE desperate to rid your garden of burrowing rabbits and squirrels, collect some hair from your local hairdresser and once a month work some into the soil of your flowerbed.

PLANT CHIVES AT the base of a gooseberry bush to keep saw flies away.

❋ ❋ ❋

FRENCH AND AFRICAN marigolds have a pungent smell and will deter black fly if planted around susceptible plants.

❋ ❋ ❋

FED UP WITH earwigs in your dahlias? Placing a flowerpot filled with crumpled up tissue upside down on a stick will tempt the earwigs away to a new home.

Keep the neighbours' cats
away from your plants with
lemon and orange peel or a
good sprinkling of pepper!

PROTECT AGAINST RODENTS by covering newly bedded plants with a layer of holly leaves.

✽ ✽ ✽

ANOTHER WAY TO frighten cats away is by placing a small length of hosepipe in amongst your plants – the cats will think that it's a snake!

IF A CAT is extremely bold and just won't keep away from your garden, a blast from your hose should do the trick nicely.

※ ※ ※

DETER MICE FROM invading your garden by spreading mint around the borders.

※ ※ ※

STICK OPEN BOTTLES into molehills, as the sound of wind blowing over the empty bottle tops will scare the moles away.

PROTECT YOURSELF FROM gnats in the garden by rubbing vanilla extract or fresh mint onto your skin.

❈ ❈ ❈

GOOD NEWS IF you live near a pond or river – ducks consider slugs quite a delicacy!

Garden Lore...

A sliced onion pressed onto an insect bite relieves the itch and prevents swelling.

Water, Water, Everywhere

'Water is the driver of nature.'

Leonardo da Vinci

WHEN BUILDING A new pond, place it in a lightly shaded area, as the sun encourages the growth of algae.

🌿 🌿 🌿

INCORPORATE AN OVERFLOW pipe to prevent the pond from overflowing in heavy rainfall.

🌿 🌿 🌿

CUT THE LEGS off your old tights and use them to plant around your pond. Fill the tights with aquatic compost and then tie a knot in the end. After burning some holes and plant your aquatic plants through them, position the bag around the edge of your pond. Don't worry about how the bulging tights look, the plants will soon grow and cover them up!

SUBMERGE AQUATIC PLANTS in your pond to help to clean and oxygenate the water. Ask at your garden centre for species of *myriophyllum* (parrot feather).

✹ ✹ ✹

MAKE LIFE DIFFICULT for marauding herons by restricting their access to your pond – plant shrubs right up to the edge.

✹ ✹ ✹

INCLUDE A FOUNTAIN or waterfall in your pond to prevent the water from stagnating, although not if you have water lilies as they will not appreciate the constant disruption.

IF YOU DON'T have room for a pond in your garden, create a small water feature out of half a barrel or even an old kitchen sink.

❧ ❧ ❧

DON'T BE TOO impatient when it comes to introducing new fish to your pond – keep the fish in their plastic bag and float it unopened on the pond until the temperature of the water in the bag matches that in the pond. Then give the fish a little taster of the pond water in their bag before gently releasing them into the pond.

❧ ❧ ❧

NEVER CHANGE THE water in your pond as this will affect the balance of life in it. Replant every five to ten years, but apart from this leave the pond to its own devices.

ON THOSE COLD nights, leave a football bobbing around in the pond to stop it from completely freezing over. When you remove the ball in the morning (you may need the assistance of some boiling water!) there will be an airhole for your fish.

※ ※ ※

IN THE EVENT that your pond does freeze over, do not strike a blow to break up the ice if you have fish, as the shock can kill the poor blighters! Fill a plastic bottle with hot water and leave on the ice to thaw it out.

DON'T THROW AWAY any algae that you remove – chuck it on the compost pile.

※ ※ ※

COVER YOUR POND with a sturdy net when there are small things around – children, young pets, hedgehogs, or anything else likely to take a tumble!

Garden Lore...

A bunch of violets worn around the neck will protect the wearer against drunkenness!

Accessorise!
Accessorise!
Accessorise!

'To sit in the shade on a fine day and look upon verdure is the most perfect refreshment.'

Jane Austen

IF YOUR PLASTIC garden furniture is stained and tired looking, make a paste of baking soda and water and rub it on the furniture. Wipe off after a few minutes and your furniture will have a new lease of life.

❀ ❀ ❀

MAKE STONEWORK LOOK older and more natural by rubbing live yoghurt over it to create algae. Alternatively, you could rub soot into the crevices.

111

ALUMINIUM FURNITURE AND metal tools can be protected over the winter months by smearing cooking oil over them. Remember to wipe off the oil before using them again.

❈ ❈ ❈

ROUGHEN SURFACES OF stonework to encourage lichen and moss to grow.

❈ ❈ ❈

IF YOUR WICKER garden furniture has become saggy and sorry, turn it upside down, pour boiling salted water over it and leave it to dry in the sun on a hot day.

BROWSE AROUND SCRAPYARDS for unconventional plant containers such as chimney pots, barrels and coal scuttles.

❋ ❋ ❋

FOR A QUICK way to clean your barbecue grill, simply rub the grill in some sand. This will remove most of the grease. All you have to do then is hose it down!

Garden Lore...

Hiding in the branches of a yew tree makes you invisible.

The Fruits of your Labours

'What was paradise, but a garden full of vegetables and herbs and pleasure? Nothing there but delights.'

William Lawson

ROTATE YOUR VEGETABLES yearly to prevent a serious build up of nasty pests and diseases.

❦ ❦ ❦

KEEP YOUR VEGETABLE plot weed free. Weeds are particularly nasty things in a vegetable garden as they steal the vegetables' water, nutrients, space and light, and they also harbour pests and spread diseases.

❦ ❦ ❦

CONSTANT PICKING KEEPS runner beans producing continually.

WHEN YOU CUT a cabbage, make two nicks crosswise on the top of the stump, and within a month or six weeks it will sprout again and give you a crop of tender greens.

※ ※ ※

BEETROOTS HATE CROWDS – sow them in rows about seven inches apart.

※ ※ ※

DISSOLVE 450 GRAMS of dried milk in a little hot water and then add to 5 litres of cold water. Spray on tomatoes, lettuce and cucumber when planting and then every ten days afterwards to help growth.

Garlic, leeks and shallots take up little space, have shallow roots and have few insect or disease problems.

TEST IF YOUR sweetcorn is ready to eat when the tassels turn brown. Peel back the sheath covering the cob and press a niblet with your fingernail – if there's a creamy liquid then it's ready!

❁ ❁ ❁

TO PREVENT CLUB root in cabbages, bury sticks of rhubarb when planting out your cabbage seedlings. Rhubarb contains oxalic acid that deters the enzymes that cause club root.

SOW RESISTANT VARIETIES of carrot, such as Nantes and Amsterdam, in February and March and then again in June. This will baffle pesky carrot flies.

※ ※ ※

UNLESS YOU LIKE misshapen carrots, avoid planting them in very stony ground, fresh manure or heavy clods. Help your carrots to grow straight by distributing a row of ground coffee grinds when sowing your carrot seeds. This also helps to deter carrot flies!

※ ※ ※

PEAS, BEANS, TOMATOES, cucumbers, marrows and courgettes reach their critical period when they start to flower so watering them heavily at this time will increase the yield substantially.

Wait until the soil is well warmed before planting string beans, corn, cucumbers, squash, pumpkins or spinach seed.

✿ ✿ ✿

Harvest onion bulbs when the tops have fallen over. Remove them from the ground and clean away any soil before storing them in a cool dry place.

THE LARGER THE vegetable seed, the deeper it should be sown. Roughly speaking, smaller seeds such as onions, lettuces, and carrots should be sown about half an inch deep, whereas larger seeds such as cabbages should be one inch deep and beans two inches deep.

❋ ❋ ❋

INCREASE THE SIZE of your artichoke heads by making two incisions in the fully developed stalk just below the head and inserting two criss-crossing matchsticks.

❋ ❋ ❋

SOW YOUR TENDER vegetables such as tomatoes, peppers and cucumbers indoors, along with any plants that have a long growing season and so require early planting, such as celery and onions.

A LARGE NUMBER of salad greens do better in cool conditions. Help them by planting them in the shade of taller plants and flowers.

❈ ❈ ❈

GROW RASPBERRIES ALONG a trellis to facilitate picking. Trellis support also keeps the fruit off the ground making it cleaner and giving easy access to light.

❈ ❈ ❈

INCREASE THE YIELD of your fruit trees by scattering bonfire ash around their bases in March.

A GRAPEVINE CAN make a beautiful cover for a pergola – make sure you grow it in a sunny place with rich compost and good drainage. Don't forget to water it liberally.

✹ ✹ ✹

THE IDEAL TIME for picking fruit for jam is when it is *just* ripe.

CHECK TO SEE how ripe an apple is by gently lifting it in the palm of your hand while it is still attached to the tree. When it is ripe for plucking, the stalk will detach itself easily.

Garden Lore...

If you cut an apple in half and count how many seeds are inside, you will know how many children you will have.

Keeping your Garden Growing

*'The secret of improved plant breeding,
apart from scientific knowledge, is love.'*

Luther Burbank

WHEN RAKING LEAVES into a pile, watering them lightly to make them soggy will ensure that the leaves will not blow away in the wind.

❀ ❀ ❀

DO NOT CUT all branches of a shrub to a uniform length as this can result in unnatural growth. Instead, prune a shrub by cutting selected branches to ground level.

DON'T BE AFRAID to be drastic when pruning newly planted roses – by chopping them down to three inches, you will build a strong foundation for vigorous growth.

✿ ✿ ✿

DEADHEADING IS CUTTING off ugly old flower heads that have already bloomed. When you deadhead, be sure to cut just above a leaf node (knobbly bit), where new growth can begin. Deadheading promotes new growth and budding, and makes the plants look tidier.

✿ ✿ ✿

PRUNE EARLY BLOOMING plants, such as lilacs and azaleas, after the flowers fade so the plant will have time to set buds for next year.

THERE ARE SOME summer bloomers that bloom better and look neater if cut back in spring. These include Japanese spirea, potentilla and 'Annabelle' hydrangea.

✳ ✳ ✳

DO NOT TWIST and turn the shears when pruning as this will damage both the plant and the shears.

✳ ✳ ✳

CUT THE SHOOT about six millimetres above a bud, cutting diagonally down and away from the bud to encourage bushier growth.

DO NOT CUT a daffodil as soon as the flower dies. Loop the leaves together until they dry out as this will help supply food to the bud for next year.

※ ※ ※

KEEP HEDGES SLIGHTLY thicker at the bottom when pruning to help maintain the foliage near the ground.

※ ※ ※

IF YOUR OLD leaves are droopy, the most likely cause is under-watering, whereas when younger plant leaves turn yellow, it's usually caused by over-watering.

IF YOU HAVE plants that suffer in dry weather, such as hydrangeas, insert a plastic pipe vertically into the ground near the plant when you first plant it. Pour water down this pipe to get more moisture to the roots and cheer up your thirsty plants!

Garden Lore...

If you catch a falling leaf on the first day of autumn you will not catch a cold all winter.

Weed 'em out

SOAK THE GROUND before pulling up weeds, as this will make the job a lot easier.

❈ ❈ ❈

A TEASPOONFUL OF salt applied directly to a weed in your lawn will kill it. Alternatively, spray weeds with vinegar on a sunny day.

❈ ❈ ❈

KILL WEEDS ON gravel walks and in between paving stones with a concoction of boiling water and salt.

DO NOT HOE in moist conditions as this may divide and spread the weeds. Hoe in dry, sunny conditions if possible.

※ ※ ※

WHEN HOEING THE ground, only disturb the top half inch of soil, as going deeper than this will cause more weed seeds to germinate.

※ ※ ※

SEVER DEEP-ROOTED PERENNIALS, such as dandelions and docks, as far down in the ground as possible with a long bladed knife.

CONTROL WEEDS ON your lawn by using a selective weedkiller but try not to cut the grass for at least a week after application, and never put infected grass clippings on your compost heap.

✿ ✿ ✿

JAPANESE KNOTWEED IS a stubborn so-and-so, and is almost impossible to eradicate. The stems are hollow so once you've cut them back, pour weedkiller down them to halt the growth. Then dig a solid barrier round the stems to stop the roots from spreading and continue to douse the weed with weedkiller every time it recovers.

IF YOUR WEEDS keep coming back – learn to love them! Many weeds bring birds and other wildlife into your garden because of the insects they attract.

Garden Lore...

Clover protects human beings and animals from the spell of magicians and the wiles of fairies, and brings good luck to those who keep it in the house.

Say it with Flowers

*'I'd rather have roses on my table
than diamonds on my neck.'*

Emma Goldman

PICK FLOWERS BEFORE the buds have opened, in the early morning or late in the evening. This is when they will be at their freshest.

❈ ❈ ❈

CUT THE BOTTOM couple of inches from the stems of flowers underwater so that the maximum amount of moisture can reach the stems without an airlock.

❈ ❈ ❈

PUT PINPRICKS IN a tulip's stem just below the flower head to prevent them from drooping too quickly.

Poppies will last that little
bit longer if you singe the
base of their stems with a
candle or cigarette lighter
before arranging them.

CUT LILY STEMS at an angle and store them up to their necks in a bucket of water for an hour before arranging them.

✿ ✿ ✿

BEFORE ARRANGING HYDRANGEAS or violets in a vase, leave them upside down in a bowl of water for a few minutes to ensure that the flower lasts longer – their heads are absorbent.

CARNATIONS ARE ONE of the longest lasting of all flowers. Cut the stems underwater, in between two nodes and leave in a bucketful of water for an hour or so before arranging them.

✿ ✿ ✿

STRIP THE BOTTOM leaves from cut flowers before placing them in a container as leaves below the water level make the water smelly and slimy.

✿ ✿ ✿

GET EXTRA MILEAGE out of your flowers by cutting half an inch from their stems when they start to look a bit sorry and plunging the trimmed stems immediately into boiling water before putting the flowers straight back into a vase of cold water.

To REVIVE DROOPY flowers, drop an aspirin or two into the vase. A copper penny in the water will also do the trick.

✿ ✿ ✿

MAKE YOUR FLOWERS last longer in a warm room by adding a couple of ice cubes to the vase every day.

PROLONG THE LIFE of a cut flower decoration by adding the odd foxglove, as these protect against diseases. Remember that foxgloves are poisonous though!

✳ ✳ ✳

APPLES EMIT A gas that is harmful to carnations so keep them well apart!

✳ ✳ ✳

GIVE YOUR FLOWERS a little assistance standing up straight by adding starch to the water.

DO NOT PUT daffodils and tulips in the same container, as this will shorten their life.

※ ※ ※

ADD SALT TO a vase of tulips to stop their heads opening fully and extend their life.

※ ※ ※

DEAD FLOWERS EMIT gases that affect their healthier vase-mates, so always make sure that you remove them.

ADD A TEASPOONFUL of household bleach to a vase of flowers to prevent the water from becoming cloudy.

Garden Lore...

The Irish believe that picking a foxglove will offend the fairies that live within the flowers and will bring bad luck to the picker and their family.

Around the House

'God made rainy days so gardeners
could get the housework done.'

Anonymous

IF YOU ARE a novice house gardener, buy easy-peasy plants such as spider plants, *sansevieria* (mother-in-law's tongue), peace lilies and *tradescantia*.

🌸 🌸 🌸

WHEN CHOOSING WHICH house plants to buy, avoid ones which have been sitting outside or in a doorway, as such factors will have an ill effect on the poor plants.

🌸 🌸 🌸

YOU CAN EITHER water from above or below (using a tray or saucer) – the choice is yours! Bear in mind though, that constant watering from below brings nutrient salts to the soil surface that can eventually burn the plant's upper roots or stem!

DO NOT FOLLOW a strict schedule when watering house plants. To test whether your plants are in need of a drink, place a pebble on top of the soil. If, when you turn the pebble over, the underside is dry, then give the plant some water. Alternatively you could stick your thumb into the soil (about two inches) and water the plant if it feels dry.

✿ ✿ ✿

MAKE YOUR HOUSE plants greener by adding a drop or two of castor oil to the soil every six weeks.

MIX ANY WINE or beer leftovers with a little water and give the mixture to your plant to make them happy and perky.

✳ ✳ ✳

ADD CALCIUM TO your house plants by rinsing milk bottles with water and pouring it into their pots.

✳ ✳ ✳

SHINE UP YOUR plant leaves by rubbing a little skimmed milk onto them.

USE A PLASTIC funnel dug into the soil to water house plants so that the water goes straight into the soil without spilling all over the leaves and creating a mess.

❀ ❀ ❀

FEED YOUR HOUSE plants with leftover tea, preferably while it is still warm.

❀ ❀ ❀

NEUTRALISE TAP WATER by adding a few drops of vinegar to your watering can.

TURN YOUR HOUSE plant regularly to prevent it from leaning towards the light and growing unevenly.

☀ ☀ ☀

DO NOT KEEP your house plants on windowsills at night in the winter – when you close the curtains you will trap cold air in around them and the plants could freeze to death!

PLANTS LOVE RAINWATER. Leave a bucket outdoors then feed the water to your plants once enough has been collected.

❀ ❀ ❀

CRUSH EGGSHELLS IN a watering can, fill with water and leave overnight. This will create a nutritious treat for your house plants.

❀ ❀ ❀

DON'T POUR THE dirty water from your aquarium down the sink when you change it – house plants love this tipple.

Ferns love a nice cuppa,
so mix tea or coffee in
with their compost.

TO KEEP HOUSE plants watered whilst you are away for a few days, place one end of a pipe cleaner into the soil by the plant and the other end into some water. The pipe cleaner will gradually draw up the water. This is similar to the trick for watering potted plants but because a house plant can be smaller than a potted plant, a smaller wick is needed.

❀ ❀ ❀

AVOID WATERING YOUR house plants late in the day over the winter as the drop in temperature at night could chill the roots.

PERK UP YOUR tired, pale plants by adding some Epsom salts to a tablespoon of water and feeding it to them.

Garden Lore...

In Wales it was considered unlucky to bring honeysuckle into the house, but in Somerset it foretold a wedding.

Lunar Gardening

'The moon, like a flower
In heaven's high bower,
With silent delight
Sits and smiles on the night.'

William Blake

LUNAR GARDENING FOCUSES on the moon's gravitational effect on the flow of moisture in soil and plants.

✳ ✳ ✳

DURING THE WAXING of the moon (when the moon gradually grows larger), sap is thought to flow more strongly, filling plants with vitality and energy, favoring the planting and harvesting of crops that mature above ground.

BUSY YOURSELF WITH the following chores when the moon is waxing: repotting house plants; sowing seeds of plants that grow above ground; fertilising; and planting evergreen and deciduous trees.

※ ※ ※

PLANTS ARE BELIEVED to orientate themselves toward their roots when the moon wanes, making this a favorable time for planting, transplanting and harvesting root crops.

※ ※ ※

PRUNE PLANTS AS the moon is waning (gradually growing smaller after a full moon), as the water table is diminishing and less sap will flow out of the cut ends.

TURN OVER GARDEN soil when the moon is waning, as there will be less moisture in the soil.

✿ ✿ ✿

THE FOURTH QUARTER of the lunar cycle is the most dormant period and is a good time for chores like weeding.

Garden Lore...

Plant elm trees for protection
from lightning.

Creatures Great and Small

'Poor indeed is the garden in which birds find no homes.'

Abram L. Urban

LOCATE A RANGE of feeders around your garden to give both aggressive and passive birds a chance to feed. Put the feeders in locations that can be viewed easily from your home.

❋ ❋ ❋

PLACE BIRDFEEDERS NEAR deep foliage to give protection from weather and predators. Try not to put them near fences or areas where predators could ambush unsuspecting birds.

KEEP YOUR BIRDBATH algae-free by laying a bundle of lavender in the water and replacing the lavender every two weeks.

❀ ❀ ❀

BEES ARE HELPFUL insects to have around the garden. They're great flower pollinators, and aren't aggressive. If you want these little helpers in your garden, you can make it more attractive for them by planting butterfly bush, Californian lilac, firethorn and daisy bush.

Birds are messy eaters
so locate bird tables
in a spot that does not
need to be pristine.

TOADS MAY NOT be the prettiest creatures, but they are a great help in the garden as they love to munch on slugs.

※ ※ ※

HEDGEHOGS ARE A cuter alternative to toads – they gobble down slugs like there is no tomorrow so attract them by providing tinned cat or dog food. Not too much though, they need to save their appetite for the slugs!

※ ※ ※

ATTRACT BATS TO your garden by growing night-blooming flowers such as moonflower and yucca to attract moths and other night-flying insects that are particularly tasty to bats.

LET FALLEN LEAVES lie instead of instantly raking them away. They will add nutrients to the soil as well as creating insect-rich habitats for ground-dwelling birds to feed on.

※ ※ ※

ENCOURAGE BUTTERFLIES TO flutter by your garden by planting lavender, Michaelmas daisies, pussy willows, scented wallflowers or forget-me-nots.

Garden Lore...

If the first butterfly you see in the year is white, you will have good luck all year.

The Accidental Gardener

How to create your own
tranquil haven

Michael Powell

Hardback

£7.99

This book is for inept armchair gardeners everywhere. Month by month, it gently guides the reader through the seasons, showing what are weeds and what are not (even if the weeds are pretty), how to dig holes and how to squish unwanted insects.

You too can create a tranquil haven in your own backyard that you'll be too exhausted to appreciate.

Michael Powell is a big fan of Diarmuid Gavin who first introduced him to the subtleties of concrete. He lives in an NCP car park in Somerset with his wife and two small bollards.

Pot-Pourri from a Surrey Garden

The Classic Diary of a Victorian Lady

Mrs C. W. Earle

Hardback

£9.99

First published in 1897, *Pot-Pourri from a Surrey Garden* was widely acclaimed by Mrs Earle's Victorian readership as the book that made gardening and naturalism fashionable.

Mrs Earle spent the winter months in London and the rest of the year in Surrey where her beloved garden took up most of her time. She claimed she was not going to write 'a gardening book, or a cookery book, or a book on furnishing or education' – and yet *Pot-pourri from a Surrey Garden* is all of these.

Written in the form of a diary, and with a refreshing frankness and charm that will delight modern readers, Mrs Earle intersperses her astute observations with recipes and gardening tips in a book that embodies a passion for country life – as fascinating and useful now as it was over 100 years ago.

www.summersdale.com